A Full Length Play

murder on center stage

By

Jerry L. Twedt

THE DRAMATIC PUBLISHING COMPANY

MURDER ON CENTER STAGE

A Full-Length Play

For Three Men and Six Women

CHARACTERS

HELEN BLESTAR . . *head of the theatre department*

ALICE
TERRY
MIKE
SHARON
DAVID . . . . *students*

MISS SHOTWELL . . . . . *instructor in the English department*

JESSICA . . . . *janitor for the theatre*

MR. STANLEY . . . . *head janitor for Fine Arts Building*

PLACE: *The stage of an old theatre.*

TIME: *A winter evening.*

ACT ONE

SCENE: The theatre of a private Liberal Arts College. The set on stage should consist of a partially completed setting for Shakespeare's "Romeo and Juliet." There should be arches, platforms and pillars suggesting a street scene. There is a candelabra and candles on stage, as well as a place where all the characters keep their coats. There should also be a ladder, a lighting panel, a sound cabinet, and a sheet or drop cloth. There is a telephone on the sound cabinet. The stage should look as any stage does when a set is half completed. It is important that there be enough flats so that a person can move around backstage and not be seen by the audience or the actors on stage.)

AT RISE OF CURTAIN: We see the Director, HELEN BLESTAR /MRS. "B"/, an attractive woman in her early fifties, on stage. With her are two college girls: ALICE, who is playing the Nurse; and TERRY, who is playing Mrs. Capulet. HELEN looks around the stage.)

HELEN. Can't anything go right? Where is Sharon?
ALICE. She was just here.
TERRY. Where's David?
HELEN. Good point, Terry. If you find one, you'll find the other. I knew it was a mistake to cast those two as Romeo and Juliet.
TERRY. But think how realistic the love scenes will be.
HELEN. True. But only if they don't wear themselves

out backstage! (All three laugh.)

(MIKE, a college boy, comes down the lighting ladder R.)

MIKE. Mrs. "B"?
HELEN. What is it, Mike?
MIKE. There's something screwy with a couple of those lights. They don't plug in like the others.
HELEN. Don't worry about it. I'll have the tech director check them tomorrow.
ALICE. The ghost strikes again!
TERRY. What ghost?
MIKE. That's right, you're new. You haven't heard about our famous ghost.
ALICE. Nobody's seen it, but a lot of people have heard it.
MIKE. At night, when the theatre is empty, all sorts of sounds have been heard . . . crying, laughing . . . it's weird.
TERRY. Is that true, Mrs. "B"?
HELEN. Terry, every theatre I've been connected with has had its ghost.
MIKE. This one's real!
ALICE. Some say it's the spirit of a girl who died on stage.
HELEN. No one ever died on this stage!
ALICE. Frances Brown told me that . . .
HELEN. I don't care what she told you. It's not true.
MIKE. But you've heard things, too. I know you have.
HELEN. This is an old theatre inside an old building. There are bound to be creaks and groans. Stop talking about ghosts and go study your lines.
MIKE. I'll practice my dueling!
HELEN. You don't hear very well, do you, Mike?

I said practice your lines.

ALICE. You'd better do as she says or she'll use her karate on you.

MIKE. That's right! I can see it now! College Theatre Director becomes black belt champion of the world!

HELEN (coldly). Please, Mike. All I'm doing is taking a self defense course at the "Y". Go study your lines!

MIKE. Yes, ma'am. (MIKE exits R. HELEN turns and shouts off stage L.)

HELEN. Sharon! Sharon Wise!

SHARON (offstage). I'm coming! I'm coming!

ALICE. Let her go, David!

(SHARON runs on stage from L. She is a pretty girl of about nineteen. On top of her jeans she is wearing a long wrap-around skirt. She is just finishing putting a safety-pin in the skirt.)

SHARON. I wasn't with David! The safety-pin broke on this stupid skirt!

TERRY. Sure! Tell us another one.

SHARON. It's the truth! Oh, Mrs. "B", I'll never learn to walk in this thing!

HELEN. Well, I'm sorry, Sharon, but girls in Sixteenth Century Verona didn't wear bluejeans. Come on, it's almost ten o'clock. Let's try and salvage something from this rehearsal.

ALICE. Where shall we start?

HELEN. Act One, Scene Three. The Nurse and Lady Capulet are on stage. Juliet, you'll enter from upstage left.

SHARON. Right. (SHARON runs to the UL area. MIKE exits.)

HELEN. Walk! Learn to walk!

SHARON. Yes, ma'am.

HELEN. All right. Try and put some feeling into it.

TERRY.

Nurse, where's my daughter? Call her forth
to me.

ALICE.

Now, by my maidenhead at twelve years old,
I bade her come. What, lamb! What, ladybird!
God forbid! . . . Where's this girl? What,
Juliet?

(There is silence. SHARON is supposed to enter but is day-dreaming.)

What, Juliet!

(Still silence.)

HELEN. Sharon! That's your cue! Do we need to send an invitation?

SHARON. Oooooops! Sorry. (HELEN shakes her head.)

HELEN. Say your last line again, Alice.

ALICE.

Where's this girl? What, Juliet!

(SHARON enters almost on a run.)

HELEN. Walk!

SHARON. Yes, ma'am.

How now! Who calls?

ALICE.

Your mother.

SHARON.

Madam, I am here. What is your will?

TERRY.

This is the matter. . . . Nurse, give leave
a while,
We must talk in secret . . . Nurse, come
back again;
I have remember'd me, thou's hear our
counsel.
Thou know'st my daughter's of a pretty age.

ALICE.

Faith, I can tell her age unto an hour.

TERRY.

She's not fourteen.

ALICE.

I'll lay fourteen of my teeth . . .
And yet, to my teen be it spoken, I have but four . . .
She's . . .

(At this point, DAVID and MIKE enter R, dueling with swords. DAVID also is a college student.)

MIKE.

Turn thee, Benvolio, look upon thy death!

DAVID.

I do not keep the peace: Put up thy sword,
Or manage it to part these men with me.

MIKE.

What, drawn, and talk of peace! I hate the word
As I hate hell, all Montagues, and thee!
Have at thee, coward!

(HELEN throws up her hands.)

HELEN. Enough! (DAVID and MIKE stop dueling. HELEN glares at them.)

DAVID. Sorry, Mrs. "B".

MIKE. We were just practicing.

HELEN. You were showing off! I thought you were beyond that. Leave those swords here and go study your lines.

DAVID. Yes, ma'am.

(DAVID and MIKE turn to exit as MISS SHOTWELL enters. She is the same age as Helen and teache English at the college. She is wearing a heavy winter coat with a large fur collar.)

MIKE. Hi, Miss Shotwell.

MISS SHOTWELL. Mike . . . David. (MISS SHOTWELL crosses to HELEN.) Brrr, what a night! It's turning into a regular blizzard.

HELEN. Grace! What are you doing here?

MISS SHOTWELL. What am I . . . ? Good heavens, Helen, that's what I want to know!

HELEN. I don't understand.

MISS SHOTWELL. Your message! When I returned home from the faculty meeting there was this urgent message for me to come to the theatre.

HELEN. I sent no message.

MISS SHOTWELL. Well, then who . . . ?

SHARON. Someone's played a trick on you.

MISS SHOTWELL. Of all the . . . Roger Bell! That's who did it! I flunked him last semester in English Literature!

HELEN. I'm sorry, Grace. Did you walk over?

MISS SHOTWELL. No . . . I took a cab.

HELEN. I'll drive you home. We're almost finished.

MISS SHOTWELL. You are finished. Jessica is on her way.

HELEN. Oh, no! That's all I need.

MISS SHOTWELL. You have no one to blame but yourself. You're the one that keeps her around.

HELEN. Someone has to help the poor thing.

MISS SHOTWELL. She should have been put in an institution years ago.

HELEN. She's harmless.

MISS SHOTWELL. I'm not so sure. She seems to be getting worse. I brought my Shakespeare class over yesterday and she almost didn't let us in!

HELEN. She was probably cleaning.

MISS SHOTWELL. She's always cleaning!

SHARON. She cornered me this afternoon and spent half an hour explaining all the things I'm doing wrong with Juliet.

MISS SHOTWELL. Oh, she's an expert on Juliet!

HELEN. I don't think she's ever forgiven you for winning that role.

MISS SHOTWELL. There's no need to tell me! She's hated me from that day to this.

MIKE. Was she ever any good as an actress?

HELEN. Yes. And before her breakdown she was brilliant. So, let's be a little kind. This theatre is her whole world.

MISS SHOTWELL. I still say that she . . . (There is some noise offstage R.)

HELEN. Shhhhh!

(JESSICA enters from R. She is a woman in her mid-fifties, but looks older. She is wearing an old shapeless dress and is carrying a mop and bucket.)

JESSICA. Helen! Helen! Have you seen this mess back here?

HELEN. Now, Jessica. We're building sets.

JESSICA. That's no excuse! This place is filthy! It'll take me two hours to clean the stage alone!

DAVID. Then don't clean it.

JESSICA. Don't you get smart with me, young man! I have a college degree! That's more than you have!

DAVID. Yes, ma'am.

JESSICA. And I acted on this very stage! Didn't I, Helen?

HELEN. Yes, you did. (HELEN motions for DAVID to be quiet. JESSICA notices MISS SHOTWELL.)

JESSICA. What are you doing here?

MISS SHOTWELL. It's too long to explain.

HELEN. Jessica, it's a terrible night. Forget about cleaning and let me take you home.

JESSICA (excitedly). No! I can't do that! The

theatre is a mess! The theatre is a mess! The theatre must be clean, Helen! It must be clean! It must be clean!

HELEN. All right . . . all right . . . you clean. But I want you to take a cab home. (JESSICA regains control of herself.)

JESSICA. Yes . . . yes, I'll do that. (JESSICA looks at SHARON, then back to HELEN.) Was she better tonight?

HELEN. Yes, I think she was.

JESSICA. I thought she would be. I talked to her. (JESSICA looks at MISS SHOTWELL, then to SHARON.) And don't pay any attention to what she says!

MISS SHOTWELL. Now, you see here, Jessica . . .

(MR. STANLEY, the head janitor for the Fine Arts Building, comes charging in from the back of the theatre. He is a grumpy man in his mid-fifties.)

MR. STANLEY. Jessica! Where is it? Where's my mophead?

JESSICA. It's mine!

MR. STANLEY. No, it's not! I saw you come out of my supply room!

JESSICA. I was looking for my pail! The one you stole!

MR. STANLEY. You left it out! One of my boys tripped over it! (MR. STANLEY reaches into Jessica's pail and pulls out the mophead.)

JESSICA. Give that back! (MR. STANLEY turns to HELEN.)

MR. STANLEY. You know the rules!

HELEN. I know the rules, Mr. Stanley. Jessica takes care of the theatre and you are in charge of the Fine Arts Building.

MR. STANLEY. And she has her supplies and I have mine!

HELEN. Jessica, is this Mr. Stanley's mop?

JESSICA. Well . . . he has four more and I don't have any!

MR. STANLEY. Then order some!

JESSICA. But I need it tonight!

HELEN. Mr. Stanley . . .

MR. STANLEY. Oh, she can have it!

HELEN. Thank you.

MR. STANLEY. Ahhh! That crazy old woman should be put away.

JESSICA. You can't talk to me like that! I have a college degree!

MR. STANLEY. So you've told me ten thousand times. If you're so smart, how come you're cleaning floors?

JESSICA. I . . . I . . . (Pause.)

HELEN. She does much more than clean floors. She assists me and I consider her help invaluable.

JESSICA. Yes . . . that's right. I'm Helen's assistant. Well, I am not going to stay here and be insulted by a janitor! (JESSICA exits R.)

HELEN (shouting after her). Make sure you take a cab home! (HELEN turns to MR. STANLEY.) That was cruel, Mr. Stanley.

MISS SHOTWELL. It really was!

MR. STANLEY. You three stick together. You always did. Well, you don't have to work with her. She isn't any better than me, yet she acts like the Queen of England!

MISS SHOTWELL. I think he's just jealous of how well Jessica keeps this theatre.

MR. STANLEY. Of course, praise her! She has one small theatre to take care of. My boys and I have three floors! We don't get so much as a thank you! (To HELEN.) I'm telling you,

Mrs. "B", she should be put in an institution!

HELEN. Jessica is harmless.

MR. STANLEY. She's just plain crazy! Mark my words!

HELEN. I've had enough for one night! Turn off the lights, David. (HELEN grabs her coat and begins to put it on. DAVID starts for the lighting panel, L. The others prepare to leave.)

MR. STANLEY. There is one thing I should tell you. I know who your famous ghost is.

DAVID. You do?

HELEN. There is no ghost.

MR. STANLEY. Yes, there is. I've seen it.

MISS SHOTWELL. Oh, come on now!

MR. STANLEY. If you don't believe me, just wait around.

SHARON. It . . . it'll be here tonight?

MR. STANLEY. Yes.

HELEN. How do you know?

MR. STANLEY. I know.

MIKE. Who is it?

MR. STANLEY. You'll find out. Pretend to leave, then come back and wait awhile. It won't be long. (MR. STANLEY begins to exit up through the audience.)

HELEN. Mr. Stanley . . .

MISS SHOTWELL. Aren't you staying?

MR. STANLEY. I've seen it. Some of us have to work for a living. (MR. STANLEY exits. HELEN shakes her head.)

HELEN. And he talks about Jessica being crazy!

MIKE. Wait a minute! What if he's right?

HELEN. You don't believe those old ghost stories!

DAVID. At least let Mike and me stay.

SHARON. Not without me, you don't!

ALICE. I want to stay, too!

HELEN. I think you've all gone crazy! (All of the young people, except TERRY, plead with HELEN.) All right! All right! What about you, Terry?

TERRY. I . . . don't know.

ALICE. Oh, come on! Don't be a party pooper.

MIKE. Yeah, it'll be fun!

TERRY. Well . . . okay.

HELEN. Are you sure, Terry? I'll take you home.

TERRY. No. I'll stay.

MISS SHOTWELL. So will I.

HELEN. Grace!

MISS SHOTWELL. Don't look at me like that! After all, I've heard about this ghost for the past fifteen years.

HELEN. Oh, what's the use. We'll all stay. (The young people cheer.) We might as well sit down.

DAVID. No! We have to pretend to leave.

HELEN. David . . .

MIKE. He's right!

ALICE. We want to make sure the ghost comes. (All the young people agree.)

HELEN. Do I have to put on my coat?

SHARON. Sure! It's cold outside. (They all laugh and grab their coats.)

DAVID (loudly). Let's wrap it up!

MIKE. I'll get the lights.

HELEN. Leave the work lights on for Jessica.

ALICE. No! The theatre needs to be dark.

HELEN. I always leave the work lights on for her.

ALICE. Not tonight!

HELEN. Oh, yes! I won't have her falling down and hurting herself. (The lights dim.)

TERRY. Ooooo, it's sort of spooky already.

DAVID (loudly). Man, will I be glad to get home!

HELEN. Why are you talking so loudly?

DAVID (stage whisper). I want to make sure the

ghost hears us go.

HELEN. Oh, come on! (They all begin to exit, R.)

ALICE. Is our lit test going to be hard, Miss Shotwell?

MISS SHOTWELL. Not if you've studied the material.

ALICE. That's what I was afraid of. (They all laugh. As they leave the stage they continue to talk.)

HELEN. No books tomorrow for Act Two. Is that understood? (There are a lot of groans.) I mean it! We're a week behind on this play as is.

MIKE. Have you ever thought of buying some teleprompters like they have on TV?

HELEN. As a matter of fact, yes! And if I get one, I'll hang it right around your neck! (They all laugh.) Good night and be careful getting back to the dorms.

(Everyone says good night, after which there is a door opening and slamming shut. There is a pause, then the characters quietly re-enter the stage.)

SHARON (stage whisper). What now?

DAVID (stage whisper). We wait.

HELEN. Why are you whispering?

DAVID. I don't want the ghost to hear us. (They all laugh.)

MISS SHOTWELL. You know what's going to happen? Jessica will come in and spoil everything.

ALICE. Oh, you're right.

HELEN. Without a doubt. I suggest we really go.

MIKE. No! Let's give it a shot.

DAVID. Yeah! Who knows? We might even see a ghost!

TERRY. I hope not.

SHARON. Don't be such a chicken.

DAVID. What shall we do while we wait?
HELEN. How about studying lines? (The young people groan.)
ALICE. I know! Let's tell ghost stories.
MIKE. Great idea! Do you know any?
SHARON. I do! My roommate told us one last night.
ALICE. Boy, is it scary! Elaine slept all night with the light on.
DAVID. Let's hear it!
SHARON. Okay. Alice, let's tell it together.
ALICE. How?
SHARON. I'll be the narrator and the older sister, you be the younger sister.
ALICE. Good! This will be fun.
SHARON. The rest of you all sit down. (Everyone but SHARON and ALICE sit.)
HELEN. What am I doing? I should be at home blocking the fourth act.
MISS SHOTWELL. Relax, Helen. This is the most excitement I've had in years.
SHARON. Everybody ready? (There are nods and affirmative answers.) This story is true.
DAVID. Only the names have been changed to protect the guilty.
SHARON. You hush! It took place in November of 1943 in a large old house in upstate New York. In this house lived two sisters, Janice and Joan Watson. Both were old . . . somewhere in their fifties.
MISS SHOTWELL. I resent that!
SHARON. Sorry, Miss Shotwell. Anyway, the wind was blowing and a hard freezing rain was beating against the windows. (MIKE begins to make a blowing wind sound.) There were loud claps of thunder. (DAVID makes a thunder noise.)
ALICE. You call that thunder?
SHARON. Shhh! The two sisters were listening to

some music on the radio.

MIKE. Live from the beautiful Carlton Hotel in New York City, we present Flibber Flanigan and his Fabulous Flutes! (MIKE begins to hum.)

SHARON. Mike!

MIKE. Sorry.

SHARON. The music suddenly stopped and an announcer broke in with a special bulletin.

DAVID. We interrupt Flibber Flanigan and his Fabulous Flutes to bring you this special bulletin.

SHARON (angrily). If you don't want to listen to the story, we won't tell it!

HELEN. You two hams stop it!

DAVID. Okay. We'll be good.

SHARON. The announcer said that an insane killer had escaped from the state mental hospital which was located only five miles from the Watson house. Just as the announcer finished, there was a huge bolt of lightning and the electricity went out. Janice, the younger sister, became hysterical.

ALICE. The electricity! Somebody has cut the lines. He's here! The killer is here!

SHARON. "Nonsense. The power always goes off in a storm like this. Don't let your imagination run away with you. We'll just light some candles like we always do." Joan lit the candles, but the flickering light made the old house even more spooky. Joan could see that Janice was near panic.

ALICE. He's here, I tell you! I can feel it. We're going to die!

SHARON. "You're just being silly. I'll lock up, then we'll go to bed." Joan took a candle and locked every window and door on the first floor. She made especially sure that the French doors leading to the garden were locked. The two sisters then went upstairs where they both decided to sleep in one bed. After what seemed hours, both sisters fell asleep. Outside the wind howled and the rain became worse. (MIKE makes the sound of the wind.) Suddenly there was a loud banging downstairs and the sisters sat up in bed. (SHARON hits a piece of wood against the floor. MIKE continues to make the sound of the wind.) Both were terrified.

ALICE. What was that?

SHARON. I . . . I don't know.

ALICE. It's him! He's downstairs!

SHARON. No . . . it . . . it can't be. I know! It's the French doors! The wind has blown them open. (DAVID picks up the piece of wood and lightly begins to imitate the sound of the French doors banging in the wind.)

ALICE. He's broken in! I know it! He's broken in!

SHARON. Oh, calm yourself, Janice. The wind has just blown them open. I'll go down and shut them.

ALICE. No! Don't leave me! He's down there. I know it!

SHARON. He's a hundred miles from here by now. If I don't close the doors, the living room furniture will be ruined.

ALICE. Don't go! He's waiting to kill you!

SHARON. Janice begged Joan not to go, but Joan had made up her mind. "You stay here. I'll come back to you. No matter what, I'll come back to you." Joan lit a candle and started down the stairs. Janice followed her to the head of the stairs. As Joan reached the first floor, a gust of wind blew out the candle. For a moment there was no sound, then Janice heard a swishing sound followed by a soft thud.

ALICE. Are . . . are you all right? Joan? Are you all right?

SHARON. There was no answer. Janice was about to speak again when she saw a figure slowly coming up the stairs. She was too frightened to scream or run. The figure came closer and closer. As it reached the landing, the house was lit by a flash of lightning. (ALICE screams.) There before Janice stood the headless body of Joan! (SHARON pauses.)

MIKE. Wow!

SHARON. The next day the police came and found Joan's head at the foot of the stairs and her body at the top. They found Janice huddled in her room. Her hair had turned completely white and she was totally insane. The escaped killer has never been found. (There is a moment of silence; then TERRY jumps to her feet.)

TERRY. I . . . I don't want to stay. I want to go back to the dorm!

DAVID. It was only a story.

TERRY. I'm sorry! I just don't want to stay. (HELEN gets up and we hear a door close, offstage R.)

ALICE (stage whisper). Someone just came in the stage door.

DAVID (stage whisper). Get down in the audience!

TERRY. I . . . I . . .

DAVID. Hurry!

(All hurry down into the front row of the orchestra. For a brief time, the stage is empty, but we hear noises from R. Then the lights are turned out. After a pause, a single spotlight comes up on the stage center area where Juliet will play the balcony scene. Again there is a pause and the sound of movement in back of the set. Then into the light enters JESSICA. Her hair is down and she is wearing a long flowing costume. She stands in the spotlight as if she were drinking in the sun.)

HELEN (stage whisper). It's Jessica!

MISS SHOTWELL (stage whisper). She's wearing my costume from Romeo and Juliet! (JESSICA suddenly becomes alert.)

JESSICA. Is somebody out there? (There is silence. JESSICA relaxes and begins her lines.)

O Romeo, Romeo! Wherefore art thou
Romeo?
Deny thy father and refuse thy name;
Or, if you wilt not, be but sworn my love,
And I'll no longer be a Capulet.
'Tis but thy name that is my enemy;
Thou art thyself, though not a Montague.
What's Montague? It is nor hand, nor foot,
Nor arm, nor face, nor any other part
Belonging to a man. O, be some other name!
What's in a name? That which we call a
rose
By any other word would smell as sweet;
So, Romeo would, were he not Romeo call'd.
Retain that dear perfection which he owes
Without that title. Romeo, doff thy name,
And for thy name which is no part of thee
Take all myself.

(The stage is suddenly fully lit. JESSICA freezes. MR. STANLEY enters from stage L. He looks up at JESSICA and laughs.)

MR. STANLEY (mimicking JESSICA). What's in a name? A rose by any other word would smell as sweet. (MR. STANLEY laughs again.)

JESSICA. You!

MR. STANLEY. Yes, me! Tonight you had an

audience. Here is your famous ghost, Mrs. "B".

JESSICA. Helen!

MR. STANLEY. After everybody's gone, she gets all dressed up and pretends she's a great actress!

JESSICA. I am an actress!

MR. STANLEY. You're a scrub woman! A crazy one at that!

HELEN. That's enough, Mr. Stanley. (HELEN walks up onto the stage.)

MR. STANLEY. It's the truth! She doesn't belong here! She should be put away on some funny farm!

HELEN. Stanley, please! (HELEN turns to JESSICA and begins to cross to her.) Jessica . . .

JESSICA. Don't you come near me!

HELEN. Jessica, I didn't know.

JESSICA. Stay away! You're against me, too! You all are! I . . . I'm an actress! A great actress! This is my theatre!

MR. STANLEY. Yours!

JESSICA. Mine! I take care of it. I . . . I love it. Here I can act. . . . Only here can I be me. . . . You want to take it away!

HELEN. Nobody is going to take anything away.

JESSICA. Yes . . . now you know . . . you'll take it away.

HELEN. Jessica . . .

JESSICA. You will!

MR. STANLEY. That's right! We will!

HELEN (to MR. STANLEY). Get out!

JESSICA. I . . . I won't let you. Nobody loves it like I do. Nobody cares for it like I do. I won't let you take it away from me!

HELEN. Jessica, listen to me . . .

JESSICA. Nobody will take it away! Nobody! (JESSICA runs offstage L. HELEN starts after her.)

HELEN. Jessica, wait!

MISS SHOTWELL. Let her go, Helen. She needs some time alone. (HELEN pauses, then comes back C.)

HELEN. I suppose you're right.

MR. STANLEY. She needs to be alone, period!

HELEN (with great control). Mr. Stanley, please leave this theatre.

MR. STANLEY. You can't protect her any longer, Mrs. "B". She's loony and you're all my witnesses. (MR. STANLEY laughs and exits R.)

DAVID. That fink!

MIKE. Yeah. I'd like to take one of his precious mops and ram it down his throat! (MISS SHOTWELL and the young people come up on the stage.)

MISS SHOTWELL. Why did he do it, Helen?

HELEN. To get Jessica fired. Now he'll go to the administration and tell them she's insane. And, as he said, we're his witnesses.

ALICE. But she's not hurting anyone.

HELEN. That doesn't matter. He'll make her sound like some lunatic and the administration will have to fire her.

TERRY. If she can't take care of this theatre, she'll just die.

HELEN. You're more right than you know, Terry.

MISS SHOTWELL. Well, I'll talk to President Hopkins in the morning.

HELEN. So will I. However, I don't think it will do much good. You kids go on back to the dorms. Grace and I will find Jessica.

DAVID. Okay. I'm sorry about all this.

HELEN. It's not anyone's fault. Good night . . . and try and study those lines.

SHARON. We will. Good night. (The young people

all say good night and exit R.)
MISS SHOTWELL. Where do you think she is?
HELEN. She's probably in one of the dressing rooms.
MISS SHOTWELL. What are you going to say?
HELEN. I haven't the faintest idea. I feel so sorry for her.
MISS SHOTWELL. Perhaps we should go in to see President Hopkins together.
HELEN. That's a good idea. (We hear some banging offstage R.)
MISS SHOTWELL. What in heaven's name is that?
HELEN. It sounds like . . .

(SHARON hurries on stage from R.)

SHARON. Mrs. "B", the side door is locked. Do you have your keys?
HELEN. Locked? That fool Stanley must have done it! (HELEN begins to look through her purse for the key.)
MISS SHOTWELL. And I doubt if he did it by accident.
HELEN. But that's what he'll claim. It's got to be here some place.

(The other young people enter from R.)

MIKE. That old Stanley Steamer is either deaf or dead!
MISS SHOTWELL. He's neither! I tell you, Helen, he's going to hear about this!
HELEN. Did any of you use my keys?
DAVID. I did,to open the shop. I put them over on the sound truck. (ALICE, who is near the sound cabinet, looks for the keys.)
ALICE. I'll look.
HELEN. Are they there?
ALICE. I can't find them.

TERRY. Are . . . are we locked in?

HELEN. No. We can go out the house doors.

MIKE. I'll check them. (MIKE jumps off the stage and runs back through the audience to the house doors. ALICE looks inside the cabinet for the keys.)

HELEN. David, are you sure you put the keys on the sound truck?

DAVID. Yes. You were helping Sharon with her costume, remember?

HELEN. If you say so. As many times as I've lost them, you'd think I'd learn!

ALICE. They're not in here. (MIKE begins to pull on the one house door.)

MIKE. Mrs. "B", it's locked.

HELEN. Try the other one. (MIKE races to the other door.)

MIKE. This one, too! (Note: All the house doors must be checked. If there are more than two, other characters may help Mike check the doors. MIKE comes back to the stage.)

TERRY. We're locked in!

DAVID. There's an ax in the shop!

HELEN. David, stop! Don't panic! Jessica is still here. She'll let us out.

MISS SHOTWELL. Unless she's the one who's locked us in.

SHARON. She did say she wouldn't let us take the theatre from her.

HELEN. Oh, that's ridiculous!

ALICE. The phone!

HELEN. Of course! I'll call my husband. He can bring my extra set of keys. (HELEN crosses to the sound truck.)

SHARON. Hurrah!

MIKE. For a minute there I was worried.

DAVID. I wasn't. I was sort of looking forward to

spending the night.

SHARON. Is that why you were going for an ax?

DAVID. Well . . . (All the young people laugh. HELEN has picked up the telephone and after a pause, taps on the button. The young people stop laughing and look at her.)

MISS SHOTWELL. What's wrong, Helen?

HELEN. The phone's dead. (The characters all look at each other.)

TERRY. I . . . I'm afraid.

MISS SHOTWELL. Jessica! Jessica, listen to me! Let us out of here! (There is no answer.) Jessica!

HELEN. Grace, yelling won't do any good.

MISS SHOTWELL. What will?

HELEN. I don't know. But if she did lock us in, she did it out of fear. Yelling will only make her more afraid.

TERRY. Is there a window we can break?

DAVID. There isn't a window in the whole theatre.

SHARON. What are we going to do, Mrs. "B"?

MIKE. I think it's time for David's ax!

DAVID. Me, too!

HELEN. Wait! That will be a last resort. The worst thing we can do is panic. After all, we're in no danger. What we should . . . (All the lights go out. The stage should be completely dark. TERRY screams.)

MIKE. The lights!

SHARON. David!

DAVID. Don't move! I'll come to you!

TERRY. We're going to die! We're going to die!

MISS SHOTWELL. Jessica! Turn on the lights!

TERRY. We're going to die!

HELEN. Terry, stop it!

SHARON. David, where are you?

HELEN. Listen, everyone. Stay right where you are!

(TERRY is sobbing.) Stop crying, Terry. Mike, do you have your lighter?

MIKE. Yes.

HELEN. Use it! (MIKE lights his lighter.) Light the candles on the candelabra. (MIKE crosses to the candelabra and begins lighting the candles. As he does so, some of the lights dimly come up to partially light the stage.)

MISS SHOTWELL. I've changed my mind. I think Mr. Stanley is absolutely right!

HELEN. Are you all okay?

ALICE. I . . . I think so. What happened to the lights?

MISS SHOTWELL. Ask Jessica! (HELEN crosses to TERRY and puts her arms around her.)

TERRY. I . . . I'm sorry, Mrs. "B". I really am.

HELEN. We understand.

DAVID. Come on, Mike. Let's check the lighting panel.

MIKE. Right. I'll grab a candle. (The two boys take a step toward the candelabra, then a pulsating strobe light comes up and a low feedback begins. As the scene continues, the feedback becomes louder and louder.)

ALICE. What . . . what's that?

DAVID. It . . . it's the strobe light.

MIKE. But how did it get on? There's nobody at the lighting board.

TERRY. What's that sound?

HELEN. Feedback. Alice, check the amplifier. (ALICE opens the sound truck.)

ALICE. It's off.

HELEN. It can't be. (ALICE turns on and off the switch.)

ALICE. There's no power! (The loud feedback continues to get louder.)

SHARON (to DAVID). Do something!

DAVID. What?
SHARON. I don't know!
MISS SHOTWELL. Turn it off! Turn it off!
TERRY. Help! Help us! Somebody please help us!
MIKE. Where's it coming from?
DAVID. I think from the back. (DAVID takes several steps UL. SHARON grabs him.)
SHARON. Don't go back there!
DAVID. We have to do something! (They all put their hands over their ears. TERRY drops to her knees.)
TERRY. I can't stand any more!

(The feedback suddenly ends and the strobe light fades. There is a pause, then a spotlight comes on R. There, propped against a platform with blood running down the side of his head, is MR. STANLEY. He looks dead. The girls scream.)

CURTAIN

ACT TWO

SCENE: The same as Act One. A few minutes later.)

AT RISE OF CURTAIN: HELEN, ALICE, SHARON, TERRY and MISS SHOTWELL are alone on stage. The lighting is as it was before the strobe and the spotlight came on. HELEN anxiously calls UC.)

HELEN. Boys, are you all right?
DAVID (offstage). Yeah!
SHARON. Hurry!
MIKE (offstage). We're okay.

(MIKE and DAVID enter through an arch C and cross to the women.)

ALICE. Did . . . did you see anything?
DAVID. No. It was so dark we could hardly see each other.
HELEN. What did you do with Mr. Stanley?
MIKE. We put him by the back drapes.
DAVID. I threw an old blanket over him.
MISS SHOTWELL. I can't believe this! I can't believe it's happening.
MIKE. If you'd carried Stanley, you'd believe it. What a mess!
SHARON. Don't talk about it!
TERRY. She's going to kill us all!
HELEN. Terry, please stop saying that!

ALICE. Maybe she's not after us. Maybe she only wanted to kill Mr. Stanley.

DAVID. Don't bet on it. She's completely flipped out.

MISS SHOTWELL. Well, what are we going to do? We can't just sit here!

MIKE. I agree. Let's split into teams and look for her.

TERRY. No! We're safer together!

MIKE. Haven't you ever heard that the best defense is a good offense?

ALICE. Oh, Mike! Stop thinking like a jock!

MIKE. Have you got a better idea?

ALICE. No!

MIKE. Then don't knock mine!

HELEN. Stop fighting! We can't afford it!

DAVID. Mrs. "B" is right. Cool it, you two.

MIKE. What do you suggest?

DAVID. Let's try and calm down and think. (MIKE picks up a sword.)

MIKE. While you think, I'll look!

HELEN. Mike, don't go!

MIKE. Mrs. "B", what if she has a gun? She could come in here and shoot us like ducks on a pond!

TERRY. A gun!

MISS SHOTWELL. Oh, dear!

MIKE. Yeah! (MIKE turns to exit L.)

HELEN. I . . . . I'm sure Jessica doesn't have a gun. She's always been afraid of them.

MIKE. You were also sure she was harmless.

HELEN. I was wrong! And I might be wrong about this. But if she has a gun, what good is your sword?

ALICE. He'll throw it at her!

SHARON. Oh, be quiet, Alice! At least he's trying to do something.

ALICE. Yes! Trying to get himself killed!

MIKE. And what would you care?

ALICE. A lot more than you think, dummy!

(ALICE begins to cry softly. MIKE looks at her and his anger melts.)

HELEN. Please wait, Mike. Going out there alone will be suicide. Jessica knows this old theatre better than anyone.

MIKE. Then what should we do?

HELEN. I'm going to try and talk to her.

MISS SHOTWELL. Talk to her? How?

HELEN. Just talk.

TERRY. Do you think she can hear us?

HELEN. Of course she can. But, I don't know if she'll answer. (Pause.) Jessica? Jessica, this is Helen. Open the doors so that the young people can go. Then you and I can sit down and talk. Don't kill any more. I know you don't want to. Trust me, Jessica. Let me help you. Please let me help you. (HELEN listens for an answer, but none comes.) Jessica, answer me! Let me help you. (There is no answer.)

MISS SHOTWELL. It's no use. She wants to kill us all.

TERRY. Oh, no . . . no!

MIKE. I'm going. I can sneak up on her.

DAVID. Wait! The ax! I forgot about the ax!

HELEN. You're right! And there's a wrecking bar!

MIKE. Grab a candle, David! Let's get'em!

(DAVID picks up the other sword and takes one of the candles.)

SHARON. Be careful.

DAVID. Don't worry. That crazy old lady can't get both of us.

HELEN. Watch yourselves.

MIKE. We will. (The boys exit L. The women watch them and keep their attention on their progress.)

TERRY. I . . . I wish they hadn't left us.
ALICE. Don't be so chicken, Terry.
SHARON. Yes, they're the ones in danger.

(At this point we should see a figure sneak onto the stage, R. It is MR. STANLEY, dressed in Jessica's long gown and wearing a wig that is styled the same as Jessica's hair. He is also wearing the "comic" stage mask. During the following dialogue, he makes his way toward the women by moving from one archway and flat to another. It is important that he be always in the shadow and that the audience think that it is Jessica. There is a noise of a falling object from L.)

HELEN. Boys! Are you all right?
DAVID (offstage). We're okay!
MIKE (offstage). I tripped over a stool!
SHARON. Where are you?
DAVID. About half way to the shop!
MISS SHOTWELL. I . . . I think I'm going to faint.
HELEN. Don't you dare!
MISS SHOTWELL. Well, I'm not doing it on purpose.
HELEN. Just sit down! We don't want to have to carry you!
MISS SHOTWELL (sitting). Oh, dear . . . oh, dear, oh, dear. . . . (MR. STANLEY makes a small noise as he moves. TERRY jumps.)
TERRY. What was that?
ALICE. What? I didn't hear anything.
SHARON. Neither did I.
TERRY. Over there . . . around the balcony.
SHARON. Did you hear a noise, Mrs. "B"?
HELEN. No. Did you, Grace?
MISS SHOTWELL. I . . . I might have . . . I don't know.

DAVID (offstage). We're at the shop!

HELEN. Good! (The feedback begins and slowly builds.)

TERRY. It's that sound again! (TERRY jumps to her feet and is about to run.)

HELEN. Terry, don't run! (ALICE grabs TERRY and holds on to her. TERRY begins to sob. SHARON takes a step back toward a pillar. The audience must know that MR. STANLEY is behind the pillar.)

ALICE. It's just feedback! That's all it is.

MIKE (offstage). What's happening?

HELEN. Get the ax and the bar!

SHARON. Hurry! (The pulsating strobe light comes on. SHARON takes another step back.)

MISS SHOTWELL. Oh, no . . . no!

HELEN. Boys, be careful! She's attacking again! (MR. STANLEY comes out from behind the pillar and raises a knife high over his head. At this point we can see that he is wearing the "comic" mask. MISS SHOTWELL sees him, gasps and points. HELEN also sees him.) Sharon! (MR. STANLEY plunges the knife down into Sharon's back. The women scream. SHARON is knocked to the floor. The knife falls to the floor and MR. STANLEY runs UC and out of sight. SHARON is on her hands and knees as HELEN rushes to her. The feedback stops and the strobe is turned off.) Oh, dear God! Sharon! Sharon!

(MIKE and DAVID come running from L. They are still carrying their swords but no ax or bar.)

MIKE. What happened?

ALICE. She stabbed Sharon! (DAVID runs to SHARON and kneels beside her.)

DAVID. No! Sharon! Sharon, can you talk?
SHARON. I . . . I don't feel anything. . . .
MISS SHOTWELL. Aren't . . . aren't you hurt?
SHARON. I . . . I . . . I don't think so.
ALICE. But I saw her stab you. (HELEN picks up the knife and pushes the blade into the handle.)
HELEN. It . . . it's only a stage knife. The blade goes up into the handle.
SHARON. Oh, David! (SHARON breaks down and sobs. DAVID holds her in his arms.)
MIKE. Why?
MISS SHOTWELL. Perhaps she confused it with a real knife.
HELEN. She has too much stage experience for that.
ALICE. Then why?
HELEN. I don't know. Let's just be thankful she did. (TERRY again begins to cry.)
TERRY. I . . . I can't stand any more . . . I can't. . . . (For a moment all we hear is the two girls sobbing.)
HELEN. Where's the ax?
MIKE. It's not there.
HELEN. It has to be! I saw it this afternoon!
MIKE. It's gone! So is the wrecking bar.
DAVID. Even the hammers are missing.
ALICE. She . . . she's hidden the tools.
MIKE. Yeah. For a crazy old lady, she sure is smart.
MISS SHOTWELL. What . . . what do we do now?
ALICE. Maybe the night watchman will come.
HELEN. On a night like this? He won't budge out of the heating plant.
TERRY. Why . . . why is she doing this to us? I've never hurt her.
HELEN. A lot of people have, Terry. (SHARON has stopped crying.)
SHARON. What happened to her? What caused her

breakdown?
ALICE. Who cares! It doesn't make any difference.
HELEN. It might.
MIKE. How?
HELEN. If we can't break out, we're going to have to out-think her. Maybe there's an answer in the story. Grace, you knew her before I did.
MISS SHOTWELL. There isn't that much to tell. She was a brilliant student. . . . active in theatre and on the paper . . . popular, attractive . . . most of us were jealous of her.
DAVID. She sounds like the "All American Girl."
HELEN. In some ways she was. But she was also high strung and nervous.
MISS SHOTWELL. Yes. Very intense. I remember times she would go days without any sleep.
ALICE. Did she date at all?
HELEN. Quite often. Although she never seemed to go with anyone very long. I think she frightened them off.
MISS SHOTWELL. She had a number of boys after her. Even poor Mr. Stanley asked her out.
MIKE. Was he a student, too?
MISS SHOTWELL. Oh, my, no. He lived in town and had just started to work as a janitor.
HELEN. I don't remember that.
MISS SHOTWELL. Certainly you do. It was while we were doing Romeo and Juliet. Jessica told me he became so flustered he tripped over his mop!
SHARON. Did she go out with him?
MISS SHOTWELL. Heavens, no! We often laughed about it, though.
DAVID. What caused her breakdown?
HELEN. Strain and overwork. She was in the final year of her Doctorate when she just fell apart. After that she spent a number of years in an

institution.

DAVID. When did she come here?

HELEN. Fifteen years ago. I found her sitting on the stage. She said she'd been happy here and asked if she could stay. So, I talked to the President and she was hired to take care of the theatre.

SHARON. Until tonight I've always felt sorry for her.

MISS SHOTWELL (to HELEN). Did you get any ideas?

HELEN. No . . . but it doesn't make any sense. Jessica isn't a violent person.

MIKE. You mean she wasn't!

DAVID. This whole thing is weird. Why all the theatrics? Why the strobe light and the feedback?

MISS SHOTWELL. Jessica was always a highly theatrical person.

DAVID. But what about the lights? The power's off, yet the strobe and that one spot work. Where do they get their power? And how does she turn them on?

MIKE. Does Jessica know anything about electronics?

HELEN. Yes. She did all of our lighting for us. Somehow she's wired those two lights separately.

DAVID. But why?

MISS SHOTWELL. She doesn't need a reason. She's insane. (The feedback begins again.)

TERRY. It's starting again!

SHARON. David!

MISS SHOTWELL. Oh, no!

HELEN. Stay away from the flats! (The group moves DC and huddles together. The sound fades out.)

ALICE. What . . . what does that mean?

HELEN. She's playing with us.

MIKE (angrily). Hey, you old bat! What did we ever do to you?

SHARON. Shouting at her won't help.

DAVID. It might. (Stage whisper.) Maybe if we get

her mad enough she'll start answering back.
ALICE. Then we'll know where she is.
TERRY. No! She'll kill us!
MIKE. We have to do something!
MISS SHOTWELL. I agree with Terry. Getting her angry is a mistake.
DAVID (stage whisper). But if we can find out where she is, we can overpower her.
SHARON. What if she has a gun?
MISS SHOTWELL. It's too risky.
MIKE. It's better than just sitting here!
HELEN. Mike, don't be so impatient. I think Terry's right. The worst thing you can do with an unbalanced person is make him angry.
DAVID. But all we're doing is reacting!
HELEN. That's better than over-acting! (DAVID throws up his hands.) David, don't be angry.
DAVID. Sorry. (DAVID sits beside SHARON. There is a pause. MIKE breaks the silence.)
MIKE. Man, this really must be getting to me.
ALICE. Why?
MIKE. I keep smelling catsup.
MISS SHOTWELL. Catsup!
MIKE. Yeah, don't any of the rest of you smell it?
MISS SHOTWELL. Well, I certainly don't! (The others shake their heads and say "no.")
MIKE. I must be cracking up. (Again the strobe light comes on and feedback begins. The sound builds slightly, then fades out. The light is turned off. TERRY begins to sob.)
MISS SHOTWELL. Jessica! Stop this! Do you hear me? Stop this!
MIKE. I've had enough of that strobe! (MIKE starts for the light.)
HELEN. What are you doing?
MIKE. I'm going to knock out that strobe! (As MIKE reaches the ladder, a breathy whispering voice

comes over the sound system. It is important that the voice not be detected as that of Mr. Stanley. This breathy voice is used whenever Mr. Stanley speaks.)

MR. STANLEY (offstage in a breathy voice). Stay away from the light! (Everyone freezes on stage.)

HELEN. Jessica?

MR. STANLEY (offstage in a breathy voice). Stay away from the light!

MIKE. No! (MIKE starts up the ladder. Immediately the strobe light comes on and the feedback becomes painfully loud.)

SHARON. Oh!

TERRY. Turn it off! Please turn it off!

HELEN. Get down, Mike!

MISS SHOTWELL. Stop it! Stop it!

ALICE. Mike, please!

DAVID. Let it go, Mike!

TERRY. I can't stand it! (HELEN grabs TERRY, who is about to run. MIKE starts down the ladder. The feedback fades and the strobe light goes out. TERRY is crying and all are badly shaken.)

MR. STANLEY (offstage). Grace . . . Grace . . . Grace . . . Grace . . .

MISS SHOTWELL. What . . . what do you want, Jessica?

MR. STANLEY (offstage). You. . . .

MISS SHOTWELL. No! No! I . . . I've never hurt you! Please, Jessica, please! (MIKE, who has remained by the ladder R, sneaks off stage as the conversation continues.)

HELEN. Jessica, listen to me. No one is going to take the theatre from you. Let me talk with you. Please trust me.

MR. STANLEY (offstage). Too late. . . .

HELEN. No, it's not. Listen to me, Jessica. Open

the doors and let everyone else go. I'll stay and talk with you.

MR. STANLEY (offstage). Grace . . . Grace . . .

MISS SHOTWELL. Helen, stop her! You have to stop her! (There is a loud falling sound from backstage right. MIKE lets out a shout, then we hear running footsteps.)

ALICE. Mike! Mike!

HELEN. What did he do?

DAVID. He snuck backstage!

HELEN. Mike, are you all right? (There is no answer.)

ALICE. Oh, no. . . .

DAVID. He needs help! (DAVID starts to cross the stage. SHARON grabs him.)

SHARON. David, wait! (MIKE groans from backstage.)

ALICE. It's Mike!

DAVID. Do you need help, Mike?

MIKE (offstage). No . . . don't come back. She's strung trip wires.

HELEN. Get back on stage! Hurry!

MIKE (offstage). I'm coming.

(There is a pause, then MIKE enters stage R, rubbing his head. ALICE runs to him.)

ALICE. Are you hurt?

MIKE. No, I bumped my head is all.

DAVID. What happened?

MIKE. I thought I had her. I got around the set and saw her behind that arch. I was trying to get in close enough to jump her when I tripped.

ALICE. Did she attack you?

MIKE. No, she ran behind the back drapes.

MISS SHOTWELL. She's going to kill me. I know it. She's going to kill me!

HELEN. Now, Grace, don't you start.

MISS SHOTWELL. It's true! You heard her calling me.

HELEN. Mike might have frightened her off.

MISS SHOTWELL. Hardly! He just made her more angry! That was a very stupid thing to do, Mike.

ALICE. He almost got her!

MISS SHOTWELL. But he didn't! He only made matters worse!

ALICE. Instead of complaining, why don't you think of something!

DAVID. Yeah!

HELEN. All of you, quiet! Bickering isn't going to help any of us!

MISS SHOTWELL. It's easy for you to talk! It wasn't your name she was calling!

HELEN. We're all in as much danger as you, Grace.

MISS SHOTWELL. No! It's my name she called! You all hate me! You want me to die!

HELEN. Grace . . .

MISS SHOTWELL. I know! You want to sacrifice me to save yourselves! I won't let you! Do you hear! I won't . . . (HELEN slaps MISS SHOTWELL across the face. MISS SHOTWELL dissolves in tears.)

HELEN. I'm sorry, Grace. If we get hysterical we don't stand a chance.

TERRY. What sort of a chance do we have in any case?

HELEN. None if we give up! But, I don't intend to give up!

SHARON. What can we do?

HELEN. Think! There has to be some way . . .

MR. STANLEY (offstage in same breathy tones). Grace . . . Grace . . . Grace . . . Grace . . .

MISS SHOTWELL. No! Please, stop it! Jessica,

don't kill me! (MIKE quickly crosses to the arch where he had seen MR. STANLEY.)

MR. STANLEY (offstage). Grace . . . Grace . . .

HELEN. Jessica, stop! Let me talk to you! (MIKE rams his sword through the flat but there is no one there. The strobe light comes on and the feedback builds.) Mike, get back from the set!

MISS SHOTWELL. I don't want to die! I don't want to die!

TERRY. Help! Please, help!

(The strobe light goes out and the feedback stops. There is a momentary silence onstage. Then MR. STANLEY, dressed in the long gown, wig, and mask suddenly becomes visible. He tosses what seems to be a stick of dynamite. The other characters look in horror at the burning fuse and MR. STANLEY disappears.)

DAVID. Dynamite!

HELEN. Get down! (HELEN, DAVID and ALICE lie down on the floor. The other women scream and cover their faces. MIKE makes a dash for the dynamite but before he can get to it, a small firecracker goes off. For a moment the stage is silent.)

ALICE. It . . . it was another trick. (MIKE bends to pick up the dynamite.)

HELEN. Don't pick it up, Mike. (MIKE pauses for a moment, then picks it up.)

MIKE. It's not dynamite. It's only a foil cylinder painted red. (MIKE angrily throws the cylinder over the set. TERRY begins to sob. ALICE tries to comfort her but TERRY is hysterical and jumps away.)

ALICE. Terry, we'll . . .

TERRY. Don't touch me! I can't stand any more of this! I can't! I have to get out! (TERRY runs to the UC arch.)

SHARON. Terry, don't!

HELEN. Mike, stop her! (MIKE makes a grab for her, but misses. TERRY exits through the center arch.)

MIKE. Terry! Come back!

ALICE. She'll get you, Terry! She'll get you! (There is a pause, then we hear a loud scream from TERRY, after which there is again silence. SHARON and ALICE both begin to cry. MISS SHOTWELL is frozen with terror.)

HELEN. Oh, dear God . . . dear God . . .

MIKE. I . . . I tried . . . she was too quick for me. . . .

DAVID. It's not your fault, Mike.

SHARON. Terry! Terry, can you hear me? (No response.)

DAVID. Terry! (Again no response.)

HELEN. We have to find her.

MISS SHOTWELL. Why? She's dead. There's nothing we can do.

HELEN. We don't know that. She may only be hurt.

MISS SHOTWELL. She's dead! And we'll all soon join her.

HELEN. Grace, shut up! (To the others.) Don't pay any attention to . . . (TERRY moans offstage UC.)

MIKE. What was that?

SHARON. I didn't hear anything.

MIKE. I thought I heard a moan. (They all listen and after a pause TERRY moans again.)

ALICE. It's Terry!

DAVID. She's alive!

HELEN. She's back by the drapes.

MIKE. Come on, David! (DAVID and MIKE start

out the middle arch, UC.)

MISS SHOTWELL. No! It's a trap! Jessica will kill you! (The boys pause.)

SHARON. She could be right.

MISS SHOTWELL. Of course I'm right. That's why she didn't kill her.

TERRY (offstage). Help . . . help me . . .

HELEN. She's hurt. We can't leave her there.

MISS SHOTWELL. I tell you it's a trap!

HELEN. What if you were back there? Would you want us to help? (MISS SHOTWELL does not answer.)

DAVID. We'll get her, Mrs. "B".

HELEN. Wait! We'll all go.

MISS SHOTWELL. No!

HELEN. We have to! Mike and David can't help Terry and protect themselves at the same time.

MISS SHOTWELL. She'll kill us!

HELEN. She won't attack if we're all together. The boys can watch for Jessica and the four of us can help Terry.

MISS SHOTWELL. I won't do it!

ALICE. Mrs. "B" is right, Miss Shotwell. We are better off . . .

MISS SHOTWELL. She's wrong! Jessica is back there waiting! I won't go! (TERRY moans again.)

HELEN. Suit yourself. Boys, each take a candle. We'll follow.

MIKE. No. I'll lead, let David bring up the rear.

HELEN. Good thinking. (MIKE and DAVID each take a candle.)

SHARON. I . . . I'm scared.

HELEN. We all are, Sharon. (The three women and DAVID and MIKE begin to exit through the UC arch.)

MISS SHOTWELL. You're fools! She'll kill you!

She'll kill you all! (MISS SHOTWELL is left alone on stage. She nervously looks around. She suddenly realizes she is alone.) Wait! Someone stay with me! Don't leave me alone!

HELEN (offstage). Follow us!

MISS SHOTWELL. No! . . . I . . . I'm afraid!

HELEN (offstage). Then stay where you are! (MISS SHOTWELL nervously paces, then stops and looks R. She puts on her heavy coat and wraps it around her.)

MISS SHOTWELL. What was that? Jessica? Jessica, are you there? Stay away from me!

(MISS SHOTWELL backs up toward L. We should see MR. STANLEY, still dressed in the gown, wig and mask, slip through an arch and behind a flat.)

MISS SHOTWELL. Helen! Helen!

HELEN (offstage). We've found Terry!

MISS SHOTWELL. Help me! She's here! I know she's here! (The strobe light comes on and the feedback builds. In panic, MISS SHOTWELL begins to back toward the flat behind which MR. STANLEY is hiding. MISS SHOTWELL screams.)

HELEN (offstage). We're coming, Grace. Mike, go on ahead!

MISS SHOTWELL. Jessica, please . . . I don't want to die . . . I don't want to die! Help me! Help me! (MISS SHOTWELL, thinking Jessica is R, has backed into a set L. MR. STANLEY jumps from behind the flat, knife raised. As he does so, MISS SHOTWELL turns and sees him.) No! No!

(MR. STANLEY tries to stab MISS SHOTWELL, but

she moves so that the knife goes into the heavy fur collar. MISS SHOTWELL screams and falls to the floor. MR. STANLEY stands over her. MIKE enters UC.)

MIKE. Miss Shotwell! (MR. STANLEY runs off stage, as MIKE stares at the fallen figure of MISS SHOTWELL.)

FAST CURTAIN

ACT THREE

SCENE: Same, a few minutes later.)

AT RISE OF CURTAIN: All of the characters, with the exception of MR. STANLEY and JESSICA, are on stage. TERRY is lying on a platform near C. The others are gathered around MISS SHOTWELL, who lies DRC, unconscious. HELEN, ALICE and SHARON are bandaging her wound. MIKE and DAVID are standing watch.)

MIKE. How's she doing?

HELEN. Not good. (HELEN motions for DAVID and MIKE to kneel beside her. They do so.)

DAVID (stage whisper). What's happening?

HELEN (stage whisper). Grace is not badly hurt. The bleeding's stopped.

SHARON (stage whisper). Her heavy coat must have deflected the knife.

MIKE. Hey, that's . . .

HELEN. Shhh! (Stage whisper.) She's in shock, but we want Jessica to believe she's dead.

DAVID (stage whisper). Yes! That way she won't attack her again.

HELEN (stage whisper). We'll see what good actors you are. Follow my lead. (Pause, then HELEN speaks in normal voice.) Grace! Grace!

SHARON. She's stopped breathing!

HELEN. Grace! Don't die! Grace!

DAVID. It's too late. She . . . she's dead.
MIKE. You did all you could.
HELEN. Poor . . . poor Grace. Oh, I'm so sorry.
ALICE. Jessica's going to kill us all!
HELEN. Stop that! She won't kill any more! I promise you. Mike, put that drop cloth over her. (MIKE takes an old sheet and puts it over MISS SHOTWELL. TERRY moans and sits up. All the characters move toward TERRY. HELEN kneels beside her.) Don't try to move. You have a nasty bump.
ALICE. What happened?
TERRY. I . . . I don't know exactly. I remember running, then she was standing right in front of me. I screamed and everything went black.
DAVID. Did she say anything?
TERRY. No. Where's Miss Shotwell? (All except TERRY look at each other.)
HELEN. She's dead, Terry.
TERRY. Dead! Oh, no! How . . . how . . . ?
HELEN. We don't know. She was alone.
TERRY. Why was she alone?
SHARON. We went backstage to get you. She was afraid to come.
TERRY. It . . . it's my fault.
HELEN. No! Don't think that! She should have come with us.
TERRY. Why . . . why didn't she kill me?
MIKE. That's what I've been wondering. She could have killed both Sharon and Terry, but didn't. Yet she killed Mr. Stanley and Miss Shotwell. It doesn't add up.
DAVID. There's a lot that doesn't add up. None of it makes sense.
SHARON. She's afraid that she won't be able to work in the theatre any more.
DAVID. But we only found out that she was the

famous ghost this evening. This whole thing has been carefully planned. The lights, the sound system, the taking of all the tools. It's been well thought out. And what about Miss Shotwell's mysterious phone call?

HELEN. You're right, David. The same thing has been bothering me.

ALICE. What's the answer?

DAVID. The only possible answer is that she's been planning it for months. But why? And why tonight?

MR. STANLEY (same breathy voice). Helen . . . Helen . . . Helen . . .

TERRY. She . . . she's starting again!

MIKE (angrily). Haven't you killed enough for one night?

MR. STANLEY. Helen . . . Helen . . .

HELEN. It seems I'm to be next.

MIKE. No! She won't get you!

DAVID. Not without getting us first.

HELEN. I don't think she wants you. I'm beginning to understand.

ALICE. Understand what?

HELEN. Who she wants to kill. She had a chance to kill Sharon and Terry, but didn't. Yet she killed Mr. Stanley and Grace.

MIKE. You mean she doesn't want to kill us?

HELEN. I don't think so. (HELEN calls out to Jessica.) Jessica! If I come backstage, will you let the young people go? (There is a brief pause.)

MR. STANLEY. Yes . . .

HELEN. I thought so.

ALICE. She's lying!

MIKE. I agree! She just wants you to make it easy for her.

HELEN. You're wrong. She could have killed two

of you and didn't.

DAVID. It's a trick, Mrs. "B". She has to kill us. We're all witnesses!

TERRY. Stop talking like that! Maybe . . . maybe Mrs. "B" is right.

SHARON. Terry! If Mrs. "B" goes back there she'll be killed! Do you want that?

TERRY. No! I . . . I . . . just don't want to die! (TERRY breaks down and sobs.)

MIKE. Shut up! Your tears won't help!

HELEN. Mike, don't be so hard on her.

DAVID. Why not? She's willing to sacrifice you to save her own neck!

TERRY. No! That's not true! I don't want her to die! I . . . I . . . Oh, I don't know what I want.

MR. STANLEY. I'll let them go . . .

MIKE. Prove it! Open the doors and let us all go!

MR. STANLEY. Helen . . . Helen . . . Helen . . .

HELEN. I . . . I have to go.

SHARON. No, Mrs. "B", you can't!

HELEN. It's your only chance!

DAVID. Do you expect us to just sit here while you go back there to die?

HELEN. I see no other way.

MIKE. Forget it! You take one step, Mrs. "B", and I'll lay you out cold! So help me, I will!

HELEN. Mike, I love you for that, but what else can I do?

ALICE. You can stay here with us.

HELEN. Listen to me! Jessica is here because of me! I am responsible! I'm responsible for you!

DAVID. We aren't kids!

HELEN. No, but your lives are all in front of you.

SHARON. What about your life?

HELEN. I don't want to die, Sharon.

MIKE. Then don't! Stop playing hero! We're all in this together.

DAVID. Right!

HELEN. Wrong! I am not playing hero! I know Jessica and I believe she will let you go!

DAVID. But, it makes no sense! We're all witnesses!

HELEN (stage whisper). She's insane! Stop trying to make sense out of it. When you're older you'll understand there are many things that make no sense. (HELEN takes a step toward the UC arch. MIKE grabs her.) Let go of me, Mike.

ALICE. Wait!

SHARON. What is it, Alice?

ALICE. Mrs. "B", your husband! What time does he expect you home?

HELEN. I'm usually home by ten-thirty.

ALICE. What time is it now?

DAVID. Ten forty-five.

MIKE. I get it! He'll be worried!

SHARON. Especially on a night like this!

ALICE. He's going to come looking for you!

TERRY. He's probably on his way right now! (MIKE, still holding HELEN, pulls her back to the group.)

MIKE. You're not going anywhere!

HELEN. But . . . but . . .

DAVID. Don't you see? Time's on our side! All we have to do is wait till he comes pounding on the door!

MR. STANLEY. Helen . . . come, or I'll kill them all . . .

MIKE. Don't listen to her! If we stay close together she can't hurt us.

MR. STANLEY. This is your last warning . . .

DAVID. If you want us, come and get us!

(There is a pause, then the strobe light comes on and

the feedback begins. Into the UC arch jumps MR. STANLEY. He is still dressed in the mask, wig and gown. He slowly aims a pistol at the group. TERRY screams.)

MIKE. She has a gun!

HELEN. Everyone get down! (All dive to the floor. MR. STANLEY aims the gun into the air and fires. He then runs behind a flat. The strobe light goes off. The feedback is turned off. The group on the stage is stunned. TERRY is crying.)

MR. STANLEY (offstage, same voice). I will not shoot high again. Come, Helen, or they will die. (HELEN slowly gets to her feet.)

ALICE. No, Mrs. "B"! Don't do it!

HELEN. Jessica . . . do you promise to let them go?

MR. STANLEY. Yes . . .

MIKE. You can't believe her!

HELEN. I have to believe her. (DAVID has fallen next to MIKE. DAVID whispers to MIKE and MIKE nods his head.)

SHARON. Please don't go! (HELEN turns and starts toward the UC arch. MIKE leaps up and grabs her.)

MIKE. No! You aren't going back there!

HELEN. Mike, let me go!

MIKE. We all stay together!

HELEN. There's no other way!

MIKE. I won't let you die!

DAVID. Let her go, Mike. (MIKE seems stunned as do the girls.)

MIKE. What did you say?

DAVID. You heard me.

SHARON. David!

MIKE. Why, you coward!

DAVID. I'm no coward! It's her life against all of ours!

HELEN. Listen to him, Mike!

MIKE. No! You're not going anywhere! (DAVID leaps to his feet and grabs MIKE.)

DAVID. Let loose of her! (In grabbing MIKE, DAVID must throw him RC. MIKE falls to the floor but immediately jumps to his feet. DAVID follows him.)

MIKE. You yellow . . . ! (MIKE takes a wild swing at DAVID but misses. DAVID pretends to hit MIKE hard in the stomach. MIKE groans and bends over.)

ALICE. Mike!

HELEN. Stop fighting!

SHARON. David, stop it! (DAVID gives MIKE a pretend uppercut that sends MIKE sprawling extreme R. He should be half off the set. ALICE leaps to her feet and starts toward MIKE.)

ALICE. What have you done! (DAVID grabs her and pushes her back C.)

DAVID. Leave him alone! He's just out cold.

SHARON. I hate you!

DAVID. I'd much rather you hate me alive than love me dead!

HELEN. David's right! He's thinking for all of you! (HELEN turns and faces the UC arch.) I'm coming, Jessica. (The strobe light comes on and the feedback begins. HELEN walks slowly toward the UC arch. MIKE has pulled himself off stage. The cross to the back arch must take long enough for MIKE to get around in back of the set.)

(As HELEN reaches the arch, MR. STANLEY jumps out with a knife in his hand. He raises it high over his head. The girls scream. At this point MIKE jumps MR. STANLEY.)

DAVID. Get her, Mike! (DAVID runs to help MIKE, but HELEN steps back in his way. By the time he gets by her, MR. STANLEY has broken free of MIKE and has tossed him to the floor. In the process, he loses his wig. Once he is free of MIKE, he runs offstage.)

MIKE. She's getting away!

DAVID. I'll stop her! (As DAVID reaches the arch, HELEN yells at him.)

HELEN. Don't go back there alone! She still has the gun. (DAVID stops in the archway. HELEN collapses to the floor, and begins to cry softly. ALICE rushes to her.)

MIKE. Sorry. I thought I had her.

SHARON. You tried. You were very brave.

MIKE. It was David's idea.

SHARON. I . . . I'm sorry for what I said, David.

DAVID. That's okay.

HELEN. You shouldn't have done it. Now, she'll kill you all.

MIKE. Man, she is strong. I really had a good grip on her. (DAVID picks up the wig.)

DAVID. Hey, look. It's a wig.

HELEN. A wig? Jessica doesn't wear a wig.

ALICE. She must have been wearing one tonight.

DAVID. Wait a minute! Wait one darn minute!

TERRY. What is it?

DAVID. The catsup! Of course!

SHARON. You're not making any sense at all!

DAVID. Maybe I'm not, but this whole crazy deal is!

MIKE. Well, spill it, man!

DAVID. All along we've been trying to escape from Jessica. But it hasn't been Jessica trying to kill us.

SHARON. What?

DAVID. Jessica isn't strong enough to break Mike's hold and throw him down. That would take a woman who knew self defense or a man.

ALICE. But the voice . . .

DAVID. The voice was always a whisper. It could have been either a man or a woman.

MIKE. If it isn't Jessica, who is it?

DAVID. You answered that with your remark about smelling catsup.

HELEN. What has catsup got to do with it?

MIKE. You've lost me. I . . . wait! Stanley!

DAVID. Bull's-eye!

ALICE. But he's dead.

DAVID. I'll bet my next year's tuition he isn't. He looked dead and was all covered with what we thought was blood. But none of us really examined him. All we did was take him back stage and put a blanket over him.

TERRY. Mike had his head and you had his feet.

DAVID. Right. That's why he got some catsup on his hands.

HELEN. If what you say is true, what's happened to Jessica?

DAVID. She's probably dead.

(The single spotlight comes on and MR. STANLEY enters through the UC arch. He is no longer wearing the gown or the mask. In his hand is a gun.)

MR. STANLEY. Not yet, but she will be soon.

SHARON. Mr. Stanley!

MR. STANLEY. Don't any of you move! (MR. STANLEY turns to DAVID.) You're a very clever young man. You have it all figured out.

DAVID. Not all. I don't know how you controlled the lights and the sound.

MR. STANLEY. That was easy. I made this little electronic gadget that works like one of those automatic garage doors. See? (MR. STANLEY presses the remote unit in his hand /fake, of course/ and the strobe light comes on. He then turns it off.) You college kids aren't the only ones with brains.

HELEN. Where's Jessica?

MR. STANLEY. She's tied up down in the boiler room. It's too bad this young fellow had to foul things up. If he hadn't, you'd all be on your way back to the dorms.

DAVID. I don't believe you.

MR. STANLEY. Who cares? It happens to be true. You all were my witnesses . . . my alibi.

MIKE. I don't get you.

MR. STANLEY. Maybe your smart friend does.

DAVID. No, I don't.

MR. STANLEY. You're not as smart as I thought. I was only after the three sisters.

MIKE. What three sisters?

MR. STANLEY. Helen, Grace and Jessica. When they were students they played in Chekhov's "Three Sisters." I've always thought of them as sisters. . . . I had sisters at home . . . I hated them, too. (Pause.) You see, if you had left believing Jessica had done the killings everything would have been perfect.

DAVID. What about Jessica?

MR. STANLEY. She'd have committed suicide.

HELEN. But the authorities would have found you alive.

MR. STANLEY. Yes! That's why I needed the young people alive. When I was discovered with only a nasty gash in my head instead of being dead, they could swear that Jessica tried to kill me first.

SHARON. Why? What did the three women ever do to you?

MR. STANLEY. Why? You tell them, Helen!

HELEN. I don't know.

MR. STANLEY. Oh, how innocent you sound. But then you always were the best actress of the lot.

HELEN. I don't know what you're talking about.

MR. STANLEY. Don't lie!

HELEN. I'm not! I've never done anything to you. (MR. STANLEY glares at HELEN for a moment.)

MR. STANLEY. You don't remember. That's even worse. You destroy my life, my dreams and you don't even remember. (DAVID takes a step toward the sword that is near him. MR. STANLEY points the gun at him.) Don't you move! (MR. STANLEY glares at DAVID, then returns his attention to HELEN.) Well, I remember. It was right here in this theatre. You were doing "Romeo and Juliet." I had just started to work. It was a Friday afternoon. I remember because I was looking forward to collecting my first pay check. You and Jessica and Grace were rehearsing alone. I was out there sweeping. Jessica called to me and asked if I would come read the part of Romeo. No one will ever know how excited I was. I practically ran to the stage. We rehearsed for over an hour. You all complimented me. It was the happiest day of my life. I had dreamed of being an actor since I was small. But I had to support my family . . . my stupid sisters. . . . there wasn't any money for me to go to college. That's why I took the janitor's job. I thought I could be in the theatre and maybe . . . just maybe I would be asked to act. I used to dream that the leading man would be too sick to go on and I would step in and take his place! (MR. STANLEY laughs harshly, then pauses for a long moment.) The next day I was cleaning up backstage and I heard the three of you talking with the director. You were telling her about me and you were laughing. You told her how I had run to the stage and how terrible I was. Oh, how you laughed! Then Grace began to mimic me and you all laughed some more! I wake up nights and still hear that laughing! (There is a long pause.)

HELEN. I . . . I'm sorry. (Again MR. STANLEY laughs harshly.)

MR. STANLEY. And that makes everything right!

HELEN. It . . . it was so long ago.

MR. STANLEY. Yes . . . but it didn't stop. You enjoyed your laugh so much you made fun of me every chance you got.

HELEN. No!

MR. STANLEY. I would meet you or Grace on campus and you'd smile, and I'd stand out by the theatre doors and hear you laughing! You turned the students against me! They call me Stanley Steamer and pull their imaginary whistles once I've passed. I can see the smirks on their faces!

HELEN. Mr. Stanley, I . . .

MR. STANLEY. But even that wasn't enough! You had to bring her back! Jessica! She was loony but that didn't matter! You took the theatre from me and gave it to her! Everyone said how kind you were, but I know the real reason. You wanted the three sisters to be together again so that you could ridicule me!

DAVID. That's crazy!

MR. STANLEY. Is it? How would you know? You've only been here for three years. I'll tell you what's crazy! When Jessica came back, I felt sorry for her. I tried to be nice to her.

I thought we might work together. But no! Not Jessica! She treated me like dirt! She had her Master's Degree!

HELEN. Mr. Stanley, she's like that with everyone, including me.

MR. STANLEY. If that were true you would have gotten rid of her long ago.

SHARON. You . . . you can't kill us because of Jessica!

MR. STANLEY. You forget, young lady, that I didn't want to kill you.

HELEN. Mr. Stanley, let us go and I'll fire Jessica.

MR. STANLEY. Come now, Helen, it's a little late for that. Besides you know my secret.

HELEN. What secret?

MR. STANLEY. Oh, you <u>are</u> such a good actress. You should have been a professional!

HELEN. I have no idea what you mean!

MR. STANLEY. Don't lie to me! Jessica caught me reading my Shakespeare. She reported it to you and you told Grace. Then you broke into my house. Oh, you were clever. Only some books were out of place. But I knew! (Laughs.) I would have loved to have seen your faces when you saw my library! Suddenly I was no longer a joke! I was a threat!

MIKE. How could you be a threat?

MR. STANLEY. Because I have twice as many books on Shakespeare as the college library. And I've read them! Read them all! Helen and Grace are considered the great campus authorities on Shakespeare, but I know more than both put together! I've read every one of his plays a hundred times. I've memorized every major role! I've seen every production that came anywhere near. When they discovered what I knew,they would have to fire me. I had to act.

HELEN. I . . . I didn't know. I swear to you!

MR. STANLEY. Don't lie! You were afraid I'd show you up in front of your students! You were afraid they would laugh at you!

HELEN. Mr. Stanley, believe me!

MR. STANLEY (speaking in the convincing, well modulated voice of a trained actor).

If I dare eat, or drink, or breathe, or live,
I dare meet Surrey in a wilderness,
And spit upon him, whilst I say he lies.
And lies, and lies!

(MR. STANLEY pauses.) Richard the Second, Act Four, Scene One.

DAVID (impressed by his skill in reading the lines). Have you really memorized all the roles?

MR. STANLEY. You don't believe me? King Lear, Act Four, Scene Six. (Now he has the attention of all the actors.)

Through tatter'd clothes small vices do appear;
Robes and furr'd gowns hide all. Plate sins with gold,
And the strong lance of justice hurtless breaks;
Arm it in rags, a pigmy's straw does pierce it.
None does offend, none, I say, none; I'll able 'em.
Take that of me, my friend, who have the power
To seal th'accuser's lips. Get thee glass eyes,
And, like a scurvy politician, seem
To see the things thou dost not.

(MR. STANLEY pauses.) Macbeth, Act Five, Scene Five.

Tomorrow and tomorrow and tomorrow,
Creeps in this petty pace from day to day,
To the last syllable of recorded time;
And all our yesterdays have lighted fools
The way to dusty death. Out, out, brief candle!
Life's but a walking shadow, a poor player
That struts and frets his hour upon the stage,
And then is heard no more. It is a tale
Told by an idiot, full of sound and fury,
Signifying nothing.

HELEN (softly). You performed well.

MR. STANLEY. I could have been great! But you stopped me! You and your sisters. But now you will pay your pound of flesh. You will die on this stage where my dreams died.

TERRY. What . . . what about us?

MR. STANLEY. Ask your smart friend.

TERRY. Don't kill us! Please don't kill us!

MR. STANLEY. Why are you so sad? All theatre people dream of dramatic deaths. I'll simply be granting your dreams.

HELEN. Let them go. They have nothing to do with this.

MR. STANLEY. I've talked long enough. (MR. STANLEY points at SHARON.) You! Come over to me!

DAVID. No! Stay away from him!

MR. STANLEY. Come here, girl, or I'll shoot that young hero of yours! (DAVID grabs SHARON.)

SHARON. Let me go, David!

DAVID. No! (SHARON breaks away from DAVID.)

SHARON. Let me go! (SHARON crosses to MR. STANLEY.)

DAVID. If you hurt her . . .

MR. STANLEY. I'm not going to hurt her . . . yet . . .

HELEN. Mr. Stanley, please!

MR. STANLEY. Shut up! (MR. STANLEY turns to DAVID and MIKE.) You two pick up your swords!

MIKE. Why?

MR. STANLEY. Do as I say! (DAVID and MIKE pick up the swords.) You guys love to duel. Well, now you're going to do it for real. A fight to the death.

DAVID. You're crazy!

MR. STANLEY. You fight or this little girl dies! (MR. STANLEY grabs SHARON and puts the gun to her head.)

SHARON. David!

MR. STANLEY. Fight! (DAVID doesn't know what to do.)

DAVID. If . . . if I fight, will you let her go?

MIKE. No, David! I won't fight you!

DAVID. Will you let her go?

MR. STANLEY. Maybe . . . if you win.

DAVID. Yes or no?

MR. STANLEY. A maybe is all you'll get!

MIKE. He's lying, David! He won't let any of us go! (MR. STANLEY cocks the pistol.)

MR. STANLEY. Fight! (DAVID turns on MIKE.)

DAVID. Put up your sword, Mike.

MIKE. No! I won't fight you.

DAVID. On guard!

MIKE. No!

MR. STANLEY. If he won't fight, then kill him! (DAVID raises his sword high in the air.)

HELEN. David, stop! (DAVID pauses.)

MR. STANLEY. Stay out of this, Helen!

HELEN. No! I'm the one you want to kill. I have a proposition I think will interest you.

MR. STANLEY. What?

HELEN. Tell them to put down the swords! (MR. STANLEY pauses for a moment, then turns to DAVID and MIKE.)

MR. STANLEY. You heard her. (DAVID lowers his sword.) What's your proposition?

HELEN. You've always wanted to act and you want to kill me. Why not combine the two?

MR. STANLEY. How?

HELEN. Desdemona's death scene in Othello.

ALICE. Mrs. "B", you can't . . .

HELEN. Quiet, Alice! Well, Mr. Stanley?

MR. STANLEY. I accept. We'll do it right after the duel.

HELEN. Now, or not at all!

MR. STANLEY. If I tell you to act, you'll act!

HELEN. No! You can kill me, but you can't make me play a scene with you! (MR. STANLEY pauses for a moment.)

MR. STANLEY. Have it your way. You kids sit down and kick those swords toward me. Anyone who moves gets shot!

MIKE. No, Mrs. "B", there's no . . .

HELEN. Do as he says, Mike! (MIKE and DAVID push their swords C. They and ALICE and TERRY sit DL. SHARON sits DR.)

MR. STANLEY. Remember, nobody move! (To HELEN.) Are you ready?

HELEN. Yes. (HELEN crosses C and sits. MR. STANLEY watches her closely. He begins to lose his nerve.)

MR. STANLEY. I . . . I don't think this is such a good idea. . . .

HELEN. Act! Or are you afraid?

MR. STANLEY. I'm not afraid!

HELEN. Then begin when Othello tells Desdemona about the handkerchief. (Pause.)

MR. STANLEY. I . . . I don't seem to remember the line . . .

HELEN. Oh, come now, Mr. Stanley. You're the

great expert who has memorized all Shakespeare!

MR. STANLEY. Don't make fun of me!

HELEN. Then play the scene! (MR. STANLEY pauses, then remembers the lines and reads them well.)

MR. STANLEY.

That handkerchief which I so loved and gave
thee,
Thou gav'st to Cassio.

HELEN.

No, by my life and soul!
Send for the man, and ask him.

MR. STANLEY.

Sweet soul, take heed;
Take heed of perjury. Thou art on thy deathbed.

HELEN.

Ay, but not yet to die.

MR. STANLEY.

Yes, presently:
Therefore confess thee freely of thy sin;
For to deny each article with oath
Cannot remove nor choke the strong conception
That I do groan withal. Thou art to die!

HELEN.

Then Lord have mercy on me!

MR. STANLEY.

I say, amen.

HELEN.

And have you mercy too! I never did
Offend you in my life; never loved Cassio
But with such general warranty of heaven
As I might love; I never gave him token.

MR. STANLEY.

By heaven, I saw my handkerchief in 's
hand!
O perjur'd woman! Thou dost stone my

heart,
And makes me call what I intend to do
A murder, which I thought a sacrifice.
I saw the handkerchief.

HELEN.
He found it then;
I never gave it him; send for him hither;
Let him confess a truth.

MR. STANLEY.
He hath confess'd.

HELEN.
What, my lord?

MR. STANLEY.
That he hath us'd thee.

HELEN.
How? unlawfully?

MR. STANLEY.
Ay.

HELEN.
He will not say so!

MR. STANLEY.
No, his mouth is stopped;
Honest Iago hath ta'en orders for 't.

HELEN.
O! My fear interprets. What, is he dead?

MR. STANLEY.
Had all his hairs been lives, my great revenge
Had stomach for them all.

HELEN.
Alas! He is betray'd and I undone.

MR. STANLEY.
Out, strumpet! Weep'st thou for him to my face?

HELEN.
O, banish me, my lord, but kill me not!

MR. STANLEY.
Down, strumpet!

(MR. STANLEY kneels beside HELEN and forces her down on her back. His hand is at her throat.)

HELEN.

Kill me tomorrow; let me live tonight!

MR. STANLEY.

Nay, if you strive . . .

HELEN.

But half an hour!

MR. STANLEY.

Being done, there is no pause!

HELEN.

But while I say one prayer!

MR. STANLEY.

It is too late!

(As MR. STANLEY begins to strangle HELEN, she brings up her knee and flips him over on his back. The gun flies out of his hand and lands near MIKE. MIKE quickly picks it up.)

HELEN. Help me! Help me!

MR. STANLEY. You tricked me! (MR. STANLEY sees that MIKE has the gun pointed at him.)

MIKE. Don't move, Stanley!

DAVID. Are you okay, Mrs. "B"?

HELEN. Yes . . . I'm . . . I'm all right.

MIKE. Just stay where you are, Stanley. If you try anything, I swear I'll shoot.

MR. STANLEY. Go ahead. I've nothing to live for. (MIKE is somewhat taken aback.) What are you waiting for? You want me to get up? (MR. STANLEY rises and MIKE prepares to shoot.)

HELEN. Don't force him to shoot, Mr. Stanley.

MR. STANLEY. I'd rather be dead then spend the rest of my life in prison.

ALICE. They'll put you in a cell, all right. A padded one!

HELEN. Alice!

ALICE. It's true!

MR. STANLEY. You think I'm crazy, don't you? Don't you?

DAVID. Is what you've done the action of a sane man? (MR. STANLEY looks at DAVID for a long moment, then the fight goes out of him.)

MR. STANLEY. Maybe . . . maybe I am crazy. You kids don't know what it's like to want something . . . be close to it . . . yet, never a part of it. You don't know what it's like. . . .

TERRY. You tried to kill us!

MR. STANLEY. No, I meant you kids no harm.

SHARON. What about Mrs. "B" and Jessica and Miss Shotwell?

MR. STANLEY. I had to kill them! Don't you understand? They were going to have me fired. I'd lose my beautiful books . . . they're all I have.

HELEN. But why would you lose them?

MR. STANLEY. The little house I live in is owned by the college. If I'm fired, I'll have to leave. There'll be no place to keep them.

MIKE. That makes no sense at all.

MR. STANLEY. It . . . it made sense to me. But, it doesn't matter. I've lost everything. (MR. STANLEY sits on one of the platforms.)

HELEN. Perhaps not. Grace isn't dead. Her coat saved her. (There should be a reaction from TERRY. SHARON nods her head.) We never meant to laugh at you, Mr. Stanley. And if, as girls, we hurt you, I'm very sorry. Young girls often do stupid things.

MR. STANLEY. They . . . they'll lock me away in one of those places for crazy people.

HELEN. You need help. A hospital can give it to you.

MR. STANLEY. But, my books!

HELEN. I'm sure the library will store them for

you until . . . until you can use them again. Do you remember Macbeth's speech in Act Five, Scene Three when he asks about his wife's health? (MR. STANLEY thinks for a moment, then gives the speech.)

MR. STANLEY.

Canst thou not minister to a mind diseas'd,
Pluck from the memory a rooted sorrow,
Raze out the written troubles of the brain,
And with some sweet oblivious antidote
Cleanse the stuff'd bosom of that perilous
stuff
Which weighs upon the heart?

(There is a pause, then MR. STANLEY turns to HELEN.) Will . . . will you help me, Mrs. "B"?

HELEN. I'll help you. We'll all help you.

CURTAIN

NOTES ON CHARACTERS AND COSTUMES

HELEN: Helen is a woman in her early fifties who is dearly loved by her students. Although attractive, she is somewhat careless about her appearance. If she has any real fault, it is that she is a little slow in disciplining her actors. Helen is the head of the theatre department. A well-cut, attractive pant suit would be appropriate.

MISS SHOTWELL: Grace Shotwell teaches in the English Department at the College. She and Helen are considered to be the school's authority on Shakespeare. Miss Shotwell is in her early fifties and is a little touchy about it. She is the type of person who never seems to have a hair out of place or a wrinkle in her dress. She is much more formal with the students than Helen. She wears an expensive suit and a heavy coat with a large fur collar.

JESSICA: Jessica is also in her early fifties; however, while Helen and Miss Shotwell do not look their age, Jessica looks older than her years. Her hair is gray and drawn back in a severe bun. She wears shapeless and out-of-style dresses. Jessica suffered a nervous breakdown in her late twenties and never fully recovered. At the time of her breakdown she was working toward her Ph.D. Through Helen's kindness, she is employed as the janitor for the theatre. The theatre has become her life. Jessica is a pathetic, strange, and somewhat frightening character. When she appears in the role of Juliet, she is quite different in appearance. Her hair is down and she is wearing a long, flowing gown.

MR. STANLEY: Mr. Stanley is a bitter, humorless man. He is janitor of the Fine Arts Building in which the theatre is located. There is constant friction between Jessica and Mr. Stanley. He is in his mid-fifties but, like Jessica, looks older. He is jealous and resentful of those who have college degrees. In contrast to his personal moods, when Mr. Stanley is reciting lines he speaks with the controlled and flexible voice of a trained actor of talent. He never rants and his voice is always under control. He has devoted years to the study of Shakespeare and watched and studied presentations by good actors whenever available, and it shows. Although he ordinarily wears work clothes, in Acts Two and Three, he wears Jessica's long gown and is further disguised with a wig and "comic" stage mask.

SHARON: Sharon is a beautiful girl of nineteen. She is vivacious and full of fun, but is also strong-willed and hates to be "upstaged." She is in love with David. She wears a long wrap-around skirt over her jeans.

ALICE: Alice is twenty years old, intellectual, and thoughtful. Her tongue can be as sharp as her mind. However, she is very sensitive to the needs of others. She does not like "jocks," yet finds herself deeply attracted to Mike.

TERRY: Terry is an attractive second semester freshman who has just transfered to the college. She hopes for a career in the theatre and has a highly developed imagination. She is easily frightened, especially by the supernatural.

DAVID: David is a young man of twenty, who has

energy, drive and intelligence. He is an intense person, but has a great deal of charm. He is in love with Sharon.

MIKE: Mike is a large, happy-go-lucky young man of twenty-one. Although an excellent football player, he has fallen in love with the theatre. He loves to clown but is warm and courageous. It is easy to see why Alice is attracted to him. He wears a letter sweater.

PROPERTIES

GENERAL: Archways, platforms, flats, pillars, etc.; candelabra and candles; students' coats, purses, etc.; ladder; piece of wood; sheet or drop cloth; lighting panel; sound cabinet; telephone on sound cabinet; first-aid kit.

PERSONAL:

HELEN: Purse.
MIKE: Sword, lighter.
SHARON: Large safety pin.
DAVID: Sword.
JESSICA: Mop and bucket.
MR. STANLEY: Stage knife, small firecracker, two (supposedly) real knives, pistol, remote control unit.

DIRECTOR'S NOTES